THE ZOO GARDEN

40 ANIMAL-NAMED PLANTS KIDS CAN GROW THEMSELVES

CHRIS HASTINGS

Illustrations by Janet Hamlin

LONGSTREET PRESS, INC.
Atlanta, Georgia

Published by
LONGSTREET PRESS, INC.
A subsidiary of Cox Newspapers,
A subsidiary of Cox Enterprises, Inc.
2140 Newmarket Parkway
Suite 122
Marietta, GA 30067

Printed in the United States of America

1st printing 1997

Library of Congress Catalog Card Number: 96-79805

ISBN 1-56352-393-0

Cover illustration by Janet Hamlin
Jacket design by Neil Hollingsworth
Book design and typesetting by Laura McDonald

CONTENTS

DEAR ZOO GARDENERS:

People have their own ways of choosing which plants to grow in their home and backyard. Your mom might grow bright red flowers because they're pretty and red is her favorite color. Your uncle might plant tall evergreen trees because he's tired of looking at the street and would rather look at a tree. Your teacher might grow a leafy houseplant to decorate an empty corner in your classroom.

This book is about some fascinating plants that *you* might like to grow. They're special because each one has an animal mentioned in its name — whether because it looks like an animal, acts like an animal, or attracts animals. In fact, sometimes you might find it hard to remember whether you are growing a plant or raising an animal.

The animal plants in this book are arranged so you can choose the ones you would most like to grow. If you really like African animals, you can try to collect all of the African animal plants. If you're crazy about spiders, you can try to collect the three different plants with "spider" names. If you especially enjoy houseplants, you can try to collect all the animal plants that will grow inside your home.

When you start collecting animal plants, things might become pretty crazy if you don't start a Zoo Garden at the same time. Imagine what would happen if a zookeeper let all the animals wander around without giving them proper homes and without taking care of them. In the same way, animal plants need to be well cared for and given good places to live.

Just like a zoo, your Zoo Garden might have different habitats so each animal plant will feel right at home. For example, Piggyback Plant, Rabbit-Tracks, and Snake Plant need an indoor habitat where they will feel nice and cozy, whereas Tiger Flower, Spider Lily, and Turtlehead prefer to be outdoors where they have plenty of fresh air and sunlight. If you wish, your Zoo Garden can be made up of only indoor habitats, only outdoor habitats, or some of both. The descriptions of the plants in this book explain where each animal plant likes to live, and how much sun and moisture it needs to stay happy.

Starting a Zoo Garden doesn't just mean finding the right habitat for your animal plant; it also means that you can become a zookeeper. As a zookeeper, you can go on animal plant safaris to search for new plants, take care of the animal plants you have already collected, and take visitors on tours of your Zoo Garden. You can even decorate your Zoo Garden and give it a name.

ANIMAL PLANTS FOR YOUR ZOO GARDEN

DANDELION

(Taraxacum officinale)

A few of the animal plants you can include in your Zoo Garden grow wild and should be left where you find them. Dandelion is one of these plants. It is usually found in your lawn where it roams free like the lions of Africa.

Dandelion has green leaves with jagged edges and a yellow flower which later turns into a puff of seeds. Dandelion got its name from the French words "dent de lion" which mean "lion's tooth." The jagged edges of the leaves look like a row of lion's teeth.

If you do find some Dandelions living wild near your home, you can include them on your zoo tour and show your friends the ferocious lion's teeth.

WILD PLANT

ELEPHANT'S EAR PLANT

(*Colocasia*)

Elephant's Ear Plant has big floppy leaves that look exactly like an elephant's ears. Its giant leaves are dark green, and the stems are green, red, purple, or violet.

Elephant's Ear Plant is grown from a tuber (a root that looks like a potato) which you plant in the spring. It prefers to live in moist areas with some shade and also grows well in containers. Much like an elephant, Elephant's Ear Plant likes water, and you can give it a bath by misting its big leaves.

Each fall, when the cold makes your Elephant's Ear Plant leaves begin to turn brown, dig up its tuber and store it in a dry, cool place (55 to 65 degrees). When it gets warm again in the spring, plant the tuber and your Elephant's Ear Plant will grow again.

ANNUAL GARDEN/CONTAINER PLANT

LEOPARD FLOWER

(*Belamcanda chinensis*)

Leopard flower is one of my favorite animal plants. It has large green leaves that look like giant blades of grass. Every summer it sends up a stem from in between its leaves with several beautiful flowers on top. The flowers are orange with darker spots and look like a leopard's colorful coat.

Leopard Flower likes moist, well-drained soil with lots of sun. If you want, you can grow your Leopard Flower outside in a pot. If you do plant it in the garden, leave plenty of room around it. Leopard Flower loves to grow, and soon you will have a whole family of Leopard Flowers in your Zoo Garden.

**PERENNIAL GARDEN/
CONTAINER PLANT • ZONE 5-10**

LION'S HEART

(Physostegia virginiana)

Lion's Heart will grow well in an outside area and likes plenty of sun. It prefers fairly moist, well-drained soil and can be started from plants or from seeds.

In the summer, Lion's Heart has tall, showy spikes of flowers which range from two feet to four feet high. Since there are several different types of Lion's Heart, you might want to choose one which doesn't grow four feet high because they sometimes flop over. Lion's Heart flowers are white, pink, lavender, or rose, so make sure you pick your favorite color as well.

Lion's Heart was named because of the way the flower looks as it opens. I also like to think it was named after lions because it is very loyal. If you turn the flowers left or right, they keep looking that way.

PERENNIAL GARDEN PLANT · ZONE 3-9

MONKEY FLOWER

(*Mimulus*)

Monkey Flower is fun to grow from plants or seeds (the seeds are tiny!). Just like monkeys, which are sometimes in the trees and sometimes on the ground, Monkey Flower can grow in many different places. You can grow it in a pot, in a hanging basket, or in your backyard. Try growing it in a hanging basket on a porch or patio so your Monkey Flower can swing from a hook or rope just like a monkey.

Monkey Flowers prefer cooler areas (they grow wild along the banks of streams) with moist, well-drained soil and some shade. It is best to start them in a sunny place inside in the early spring and move them outdoors once it is warm.

Some people say that if you look closely at the flower, you will see a monkey's grinning face.

ANNUAL OR PERENNIAL
GARDEN/CONTAINER PLANT

OSTRICH FERN
(*Matteuccia struthiopteris*)

Ostrich Fern has four-foot-tall fronds (that's what you call a fern's leaves) which swoop up from the ground and look like an ostrich's long feathers. Ostrich Fern grows in a clump, so you will have lots of graceful fronds arching out of a center ring at the same time.

In the wild, Ostrich Fern grows in cooler, swampy areas so try to find a rich, moist, shady area outside for it to grow. I like to plant several of them near each other so that it looks like a bunch of ostriches standing around in a group. Ostrich Ferns spread out quickly, so you will soon have lots of ostriches in your Zoo Garden.

PERENNIAL GARDEN PLANT · ZONE 4-7

PANDA BEAR PLANT

(*Kalanchoe tomentosa*)

Panda Bear Plant's fuzzy greyish-green leaves have darker, rusty-brown tips. The leaves are a lot like a Panda Bear because a Panda Bear is fuzzy and its ears are a darker color than the rest of its body.

Panda Bear Plant is a succulent houseplant and is used to living in desert conditions. Succulents can store water in their leaves just like camels store energy in their humps.

Keep your Panda Bear Plant in a window where it will get plenty of direct sunlight and let the soil dry out before you water it again. You will know if you are watering your Panda Bear Plant too much if its leaves feel waterlogged or watering too little if its leaves shrivel up.

HOUSEPLANT

TIGER FLOWER

(Tigridia pavonia)

Tiger Flower has vivid white, yellow, orange, or red flowers. In the center of the flower are colorful markings which remind people of a tiger's coat (although they look more spotted than striped). The markings might be purple, red, or yellow.

Tiger Flower is a bulb that you plant in the spring. It blooms in the summer and grows best outside in plenty of sun (some shade in hot areas) with well-drained soil. Since Tiger Flower and Leopard Flower grow well in the same type of place, you might want to plant them next to one another so you have a whole section of big cats.

In the fall, dig up your Tiger Flower bulbs and store them in a cold but not freezing place over the winter. In the spring, you can plant the same bulbs and they will grow again.

PERENNIAL GARDEN PLANT · ZONE 7-10

TIGER-JAWS

(*Faucaria tigrina*)

Tiger-Jaws is a succulent houseplant (succulents are similar to cacti) with growling tiger teeth along the edges of its leaves. The leaves have tiny white dots and grow on top of each other to form several roaring tigers. Tiger-Jaws is hard to miss on an animal plant safari.

Tiger-Jaws loves sun and grows best in a sunny window where it will get plenty of direct sunlight. Since it is a desert plant, you can let it dry out before watering again, and you don't need to mist it with water. In the summer, Tiger-Jaws might have a pretty yellow flower. In the winter months, Tiger-Jaws likes to be fairly dry so it can rest for the coming year.

HOUSEPLANT

ZEBRA PLANT

(*Aphelandra squarrosa*)

Zebra Plants have dark green and white striped leaves that make them look like a zebra. They love to grow in bright places inside your home, but not where the sun will shine directly on their leaves. Make sure to give your Zebra Plant plenty of water during the spring and summer months. In the winter, however, let the soil dry out before you water again. Zebra Plants also love to have their leaves misted with water.

People often wonder if zebras are white with black stripes or black with white stripes. Zebra Plants have the same problem. Are their leaves green with white stripes or white with green stripes?

HOUSEPLANT

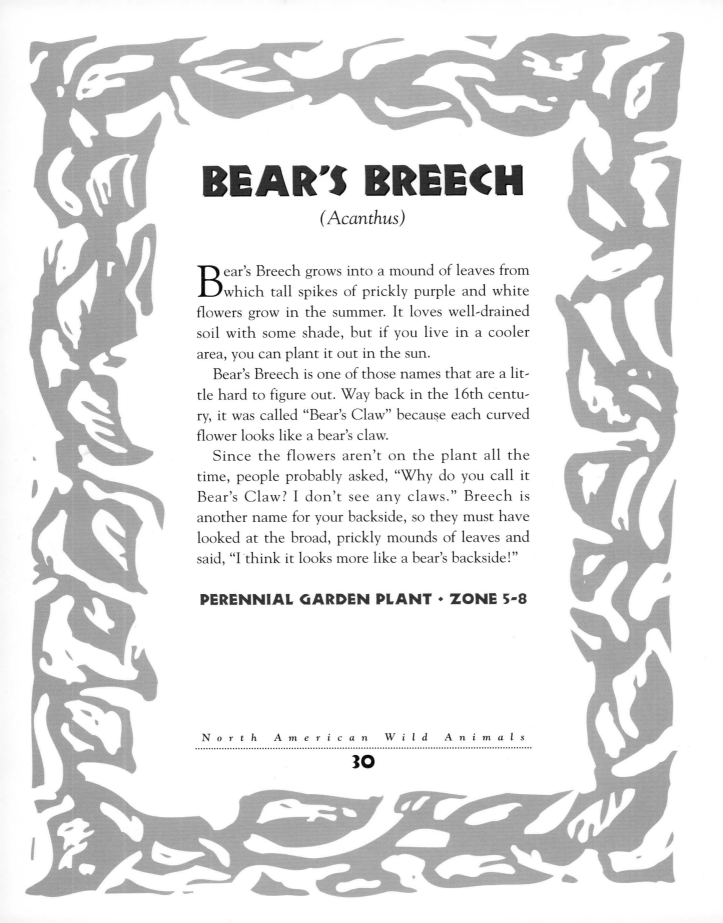

BEAR'S BREECH

(Acanthus)

Bear's Breech grows into a mound of leaves from which tall spikes of prickly purple and white flowers grow in the summer. It loves well-drained soil with some shade, but if you live in a cooler area, you can plant it out in the sun.

Bear's Breech is one of those names that are a little hard to figure out. Way back in the 16th century, it was called "Bear's Claw" because each curved flower looks like a bear's claw.

Since the flowers aren't on the plant all the time, people probably asked, "Why do you call it Bear's Claw? I don't see any claws." Breech is another name for your backside, so they must have looked at the broad, prickly mounds of leaves and said, "I think it looks more like a bear's backside!"

PERENNIAL GARDEN PLANT · ZONE 5-8

FOXGLOVE

(Digitalis)

Foxglove is a beautiful plant that can grow up to four feet tall in the summer. On its tall columns are lots of colorful, bell-shaped flowers with speckles inside the bells. Foxgloves like to grow in lightly shaded areas with moist, well-drained soil.

In England, there is a folktale which says that Foxglove got its name because mean fairies gave the plant to some foxes. The foxes then put the flowers on their toes so they could sneak around the hen house without being heard. This story may very well be true because if you look inside the flowers, you can still see fairy fingerprints.

PERENNIAL GARDEN PLANT · ZONE 4-8

GOAT'S BEARD

(*Aruncus*)

Goat's Beard is a perennial plant that grows into big leafy clumps. It likes moist soil and some shade. In the summer, Goat's Beard has lots of creamy-white flowers shaped like Christmas trees.

This animal plant got its name because if you turn the flower clusters upside down, they look like the white, pointy beard of a mountain goat. Since Goat's Beard can grow really tall (four to six feet), make sure you plant yours in the back of your Zoo Garden. Mountain goats like high places anyway, so your Goat's Beard will enjoy looking out over the rest of your animal plants.

PERENNIAL GARDEN PLANT · ZONE 4-8

HARE'S TAIL

(*Lagurus ovatus*)

Hare's Tail is an annual grass that grows in clumps and likes to be in the sun. It is usually grown from seeds, which you can plant in the spring as soon as the danger of frost has passed.

Hare's Tail forms dozens of soft, white balls of seeds which look like bunny tails. Who knows, maybe the rabbits in your neighborhood will be tricked and visit your garden thinking there is a bunny party going on.

Hare's Tail can be cut while it is still green and dried indoors in a dark, dry place. Dried Hare's Tail makes a great decoration for your bedroom over the winter months.

ANNUAL GARDEN PLANT

RABBIT'S FOOT FERN

(Davallia)

Rabbit's Foot Fern is a leafy green houseplant with delicate lacy fronds (Remember? That's what you call a fern's leaves). It doesn't like direct sunlight, and will do well in medium light somewhere inside your home. It also likes to be a little moist at all times and misted every now and then.

Rabbit's Foot Fern got its name because of the light brown, furry, root-like stems (they're called rhizomes) which grow along the surface of its soil and creep out over the edge of its pot. They are hard to miss and they do look kind of like a rabbit's foot. Unlike a rabbit, though, Rabbit's Foot Fern doesn't mind if you pet its feet.

This animal plant is in the same family as Deer's Foot Fern and Squirrel's Foot Fern. See which one you can find!

HOUSEPLANT

RABBIT-TRACKS

(Maranta leuconeura 'Kerchoveana')

Rabbit-Tracks has an interesting pattern of dark spots along its green leaves. The spots look like a rabbit hopped along and left its footprints on each leaf. In the evening, Rabbit-Tracks has a special trick. When the sun sets, it folds its leaves upward toward the ceiling.

Rabbit-Tracks is a native of Brazil and likes to grow in fairly bright places with no direct sunlight. If you put your Rabbit-Tracks in too much light, it will lose some of the color on its leaves.

Rabbit-Tracks needs to be kept slightly moist, so make sure it doesn't dry out. It also loves to have its leaves misted with water. If white spots form on its leaves, your water probably has lime in it. Try some spring water.

HOUSEPLANT

DONKEY'S TAIL

(Sedum morganianum)

Some people have another name for Donkey's Tail: Burro's Tail. Since a burro is a small donkey, you can decide if your animal plant is a Donkey's Tail or a Burro's Tail.

Regardless of the name, Donkey's Tail is a great animal plant to grow in a hanging basket. It grows three-foot-long vines that hang down over the sides and are covered with puffy green leaves that look like tiny green bananas. The vines, thick with these puffy leaves, look like donkey tails hanging out of the pot. Remember, though, that just like with a donkey, pulling on a Donkey's Tail can be dangerous (the leaves fall off).

Donkey's Tail likes direct sunlight and grows best hanging in a sunny window. Let the soil dry out before watering and don't water it as much during the wintertime.

HOUSEPLANT

HENS AND CHICKENS

(Sempervivum tectorum)

Hens and Chickens is a strange little succulent plant (similar to a cactus) which likes plenty of sun and grows best in well-drained, rocky soil. It has clusters of leaves which grow along the ground, and each grouping might cover an area about a foot wide. You might want to grow yours in a pot or container filled with rocky soil and leave it on your porch or patio. That way, your Hens and Chickens won't get loose and run around the yard like chickens sometimes do.

Hens and Chickens got its name because it has lots of mother hen plants with smaller chickens attached. If you pull off and plant one of the little chickens, it will soon grow into a hen.

PERENNIAL GARDEN/ CONTAINER PLANT · ZONE 3-8

LAMB'S EARS

(Stachys)

Lamb's Ears has soft greyish-white leaves that are fuzzy like a lamb's ear. It's a perennial and likes to spread out to make a whole flock of lambs.

Lamb's Ears likes to grow in the sun or a little shade in well-drained soil. You might want to put a small fence around your Lamb's Ears to separate it from your other animal plants and keep the lambs from wandering from the flock and getting lost.

There are several types of Lamb's Ears, but my favorite is 'Big Ears.' It is a type of "Stachys byzantina" and has *big* fuzzy leaves.

**PERENNIAL GARDEN/
CONTAINER PLANT • ZONE 5-9**

PIGGYBACK PLANT

(*Tolmiea menziesii*)

Piggyback Plant is a leafy houseplant that grows well in bright indoor places with no direct sunlight. It is grown sometimes in a pot, and sometimes in a hanging basket where it can hang down over the sides. In the summer, you can take your Piggyback Plant outside and hang it in a shady place on a porch or patio. No matter where you grow yours, keep its soil moist because Piggyback Plants become droopy when they are thirsty.

Piggyback Plant got its name because its new little leaves grow right on top of its big leaves. It looks like the little ones are riding piggyback. It's fun to keep count of how many piglets you have growing at one time, but don't forget to keep track, because more piglets pop up every week.

HOUSEPLANT

BUNNY EARS

(Opuntia microdasys)

Bunny Ears is a cactus with flat, round, green "leaves" (really stems) which stick up like a bunny rabbit's ears. Bunnies normally stick up their ears when they are listening to what is going on around them. When you look at a Bunny Ears, you would think it's trying to hear everything that's being said in the room.

Unlike some cacti, Bunny Ears has fuzzy spots instead of long thorns. *Watch out!* These spots are made up of thousands of little prickles that will stick in your finger if you try to pet them. You might want to put a "Please Do Not Pet the Animals" sign next to this plant.

Bunny Ears is a houseplant and needs plenty of direct sunlight. Let it dry out before watering and don't water it as much during the winter.

HOUSEPLANT

CATMINT

(Nepeta)

There are a whole bunch of different Catmints, many of which you can grow outdoors in your Zoo Garden. They are perennials and tend to like sunny places with well-drained soil.

There is one thing about Catmint which you have to watch out for — cats love it! They like to nibble it and nuzzle it, and they become a little crazy when they chew on it. Sometimes they roll around in it until all your Catmint plants are smushed flat.

If you really like cats but don't have one of your own, Catmint might attract a cat you can play with. If you have a cat of your own, though, he'll probably beg constantly to go outside and visit your Catmint!

**PERENNIAL GARDEN/
CONTAINER PLANT • ZONE 4-9**

CAT TAIL

(Typha latifolia)

Cattails love soggy areas along a stream or a lake. They can grow in sun or shade but they do like water! Since Cattails often grow out of control, you can always plant Catmint in your Zoo Garden and keep an eye out for wild Cattails at a local park or elsewhere in your neighborhood.

Cattails are easy to spot because they look like giant, five-foot-tall blades of grass growing along the sides of ponds. In the late summertime, Cattails form a brown flower spike which looks a little like a cat's tail sticking straight up out of the grass. Birds love to build their nests among the Cattails, and if you look closely, you might see them swooping in and out.

WILD PLANT

DOGWOOD

(*Cornus florida*)

Dogwood is the only tree in this book. Since there might be a Dogwood tree already growing in your yard or neighborhood, you might want to include it in your Zoo Garden. Dogwoods are small trees that have pretty white or pink cross-shaped blossoms in the spring.

People have been growing the many different types of Dogwoods for a long time. Back in 1640, over three hundred years ago, a botanist named John Parkinson had this to say about the Dogwood: "We for the most part call it Dogge Berry Tree, because the berries are not fit to be eaten, or to be given to a dogge." Do you think they called all their dogs "dogges" three hundred years ago?

GARDEN TREE • ZONE 5-9

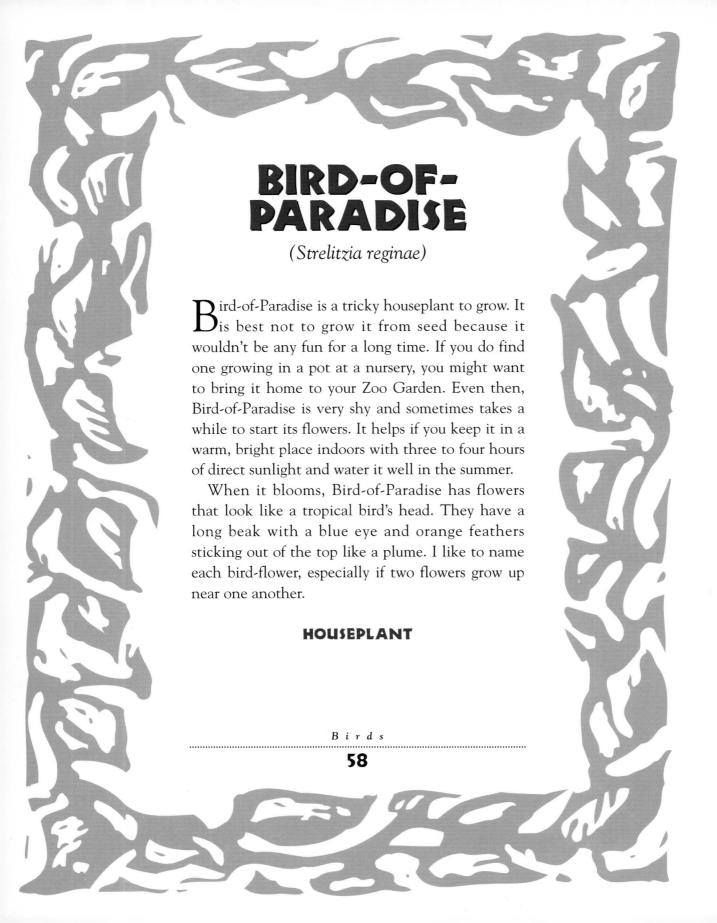

BIRD-OF-PARADISE

(Strelitzia reginae)

Bird-of-Paradise is a tricky houseplant to grow. It is best not to grow it from seed because it wouldn't be any fun for a long time. If you do find one growing in a pot at a nursery, you might want to bring it home to your Zoo Garden. Even then, Bird-of-Paradise is very shy and sometimes takes a while to start its flowers. It helps if you keep it in a warm, bright place indoors with three to four hours of direct sunlight and water it well in the summer.

When it blooms, Bird-of-Paradise has flowers that look like a tropical bird's head. They have a long beak with a blue eye and orange feathers sticking out of the top like a plume. I like to name each bird-flower, especially if two flowers grow up near one another.

HOUSEPLANT

CANARY CREEPER

(Tropaeolum peregrinum)

Canary Creeper is an annual vine you start from seeds in the spring, and it might grow to cover an area ten feet high! Canary Creeper is great to plant beside a fence, wall, or other structure in your backyard. If you help it along with a string, it will climb to the top. Canary Creeper especially likes sunny areas with moist, well-drained soil. Try to find a place where the base of the plant won't get too hot or else place some cool rocks on the surface of the soil.

Canary Creeper got its name because it has lots of bright yellow flowers in the summer. From a distance, it looks like a flock of little yellow canaries has landed on your vine!

ANNUAL GARDEN VINE

PEACOCK PLANT

(Calathea makoyana)

Peacock Plant is a little like Rabbit-Tracks except that it grows taller (up to two feet). It was nicknamed Peacock Plant because its leaves are green and beige and the colors form the shape of a peacock's feathers. The underside of the leaves is a purplish-red color.

Wild Peacock Plants grow in the shady jungles of Brazil, so you should grow yours indoors in medium light where the sun won't shine directly on it. Peacock Plant might be a good plant to grow in your bedroom.

Peacock Plants are especially happy in a pot full of moist, well-drained soil. They also love to be misted with water so they will feel like they are in a Brazilian jungle.

HOUSEPLANT

SNAIL FLOWER

(Vigna caracalla/a.k.a. Phaseolus caracalla)

Snail Flower can be grown outside as an annual vine (plant it in the spring as soon as the danger of frost has passed) or as a houseplant (if you have a *really* sunny place in your house). Depending on how much sunlight it gets, Snail Flower can grow ten to fifteen feet long. It also likes fairly moist soil and will need some type of support like a stick or piece of string to hold it up.

Snail Flower got its name because its flowers look exactly like snails. They are cream colored and they corkscrew around. The main thing to remember is that this plant needs a lot of light to form its snail-like flowers.

ANNUAL VINE/HOUSEPLANT

SNAKE'S HEAD FRITILLARY

(Fritillaria meleagris)

Snake's Head Fritillary has flowers that look like a snake's head. The flowers also have a checkered pattern so it looks like they have slippery snake scales. Some people say they look more like snakes just before the flower opens, and other people say that the opened flowers look like six snake heads. If you're scared of snakes, you might not want to get this animal plant — it looks too real!

Snake's Head Fritillary is a bulb that grows well in moist, well-drained soil with some shade. You plant them in the fall and they pop up and grow the following spring. I think they are especially fun if planted in a large group. You might want to stick with the dark colored ones because they are more snaky-looking than the white ones.

PERENNIAL GARDEN PLANT · ZONE 3-8

SNAKE PLANT

(Sansevieria trifasciata)

Just like snakes, Snake Plants come in several types with different stripes and patterns. All of them, though, have long, pointy leaves which look like a snake growing up out of a pot. The one called 'Hahnii' has wide leaves that grow up and over the pot. 'Laurentii' has snake leaves that grow up to three feet tall.

Although they prefer bright locations, Snake Plants will grow in most places indoors. It is best to let the soil dry out before watering again because Snake Plants don't like wet soil. They don't even like to have their leaves misted with water. I guess that's why they're not called Water Snake Plants!

HOUSEPLANT

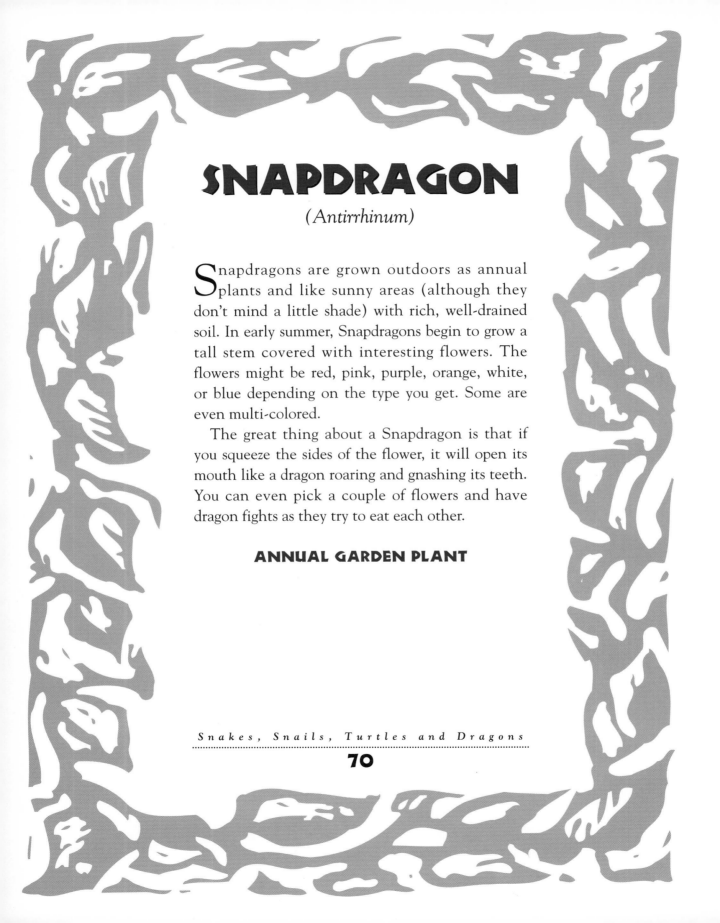

SNAPDRAGON

(*Antirrhinum*)

Snapdragons are grown outdoors as annual plants and like sunny areas (although they don't mind a little shade) with rich, well-drained soil. In early summer, Snapdragons begin to grow a tall stem covered with interesting flowers. The flowers might be red, pink, purple, orange, white, or blue depending on the type you get. Some are even multi-colored.

The great thing about a Snapdragon is that if you squeeze the sides of the flower, it will open its mouth like a dragon roaring and gnashing its teeth. You can even pick a couple of flowers and have dragon fights as they try to eat each other.

ANNUAL GARDEN PLANT

TURTLEHEAD
(Chelone)

Turtlehead is a funny perennial plant that grows three to four feet high and has rose-pink flowers. I laugh whenever I see a Turtlehead flower because it looks like a turtle's head with its mouth open. I sometimes wonder what my Turtleheads are saying, but they only seem to say "Ugggh." Maybe yours will have something nicer to say.

The best way to keep a Turtlehead happy is to make sure it doesn't dry out. They especially love moist, well-drained soil. Turtleheads will grow in a sunny or slightly shady place, but make sure to keep them watered so the Turtlehead flowers will keep popping out with new things to say.

PERENNIAL GARDEN PLANT · ZONE 5-9

BEE BALM

(*Monarda*)

Bee Balm is a beautiful plant with dozens of red or pink tube-shaped petals sticking out from all sides of its flowers. While you might think that Bee Balm only attracts bees, its flowers also provide a tasty snack for butterflies and hummingbirds. In fact, you might end up with a festival of flying nectar-lovers feasting on its flowers.

Bee Balm grows well outdoors in sunny, or slightly shady, moist soil. Make sure you keep yours evenly moist because it doesn't like to dry out. You might want to plant your Bee Balm near a window so you can watch the hummingbirds, butterflies, and bees playing from inside your home.

PERENNIAL GARDEN PLANT · ZONE 4-9

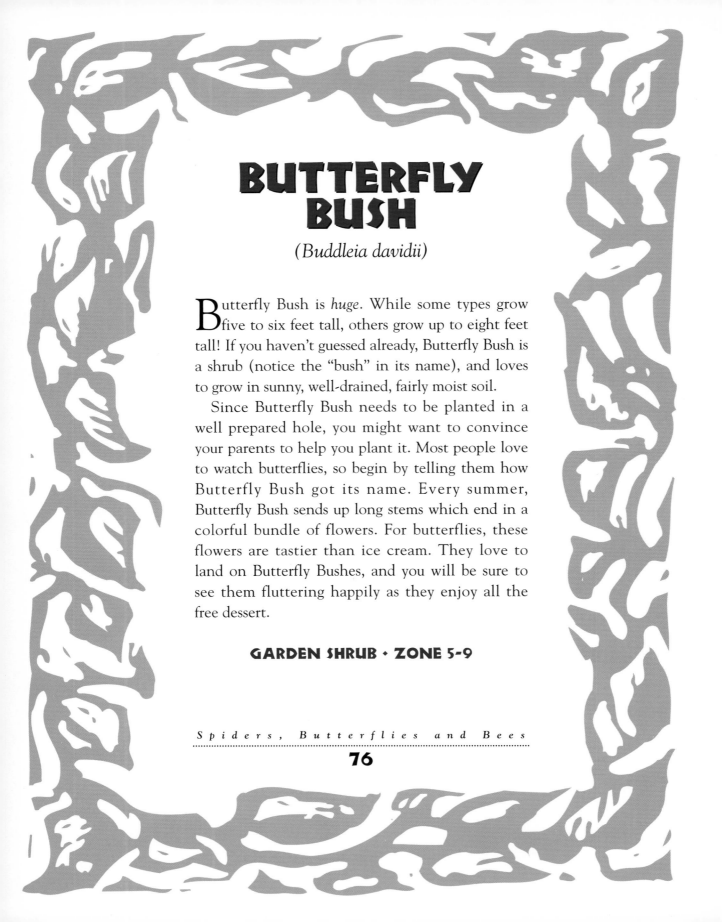

BUTTERFLY BUSH

(Buddleia davidii)

Butterfly Bush is *huge*. While some types grow five to six feet tall, others grow up to eight feet tall! If you haven't guessed already, Butterfly Bush is a shrub (notice the "bush" in its name), and loves to grow in sunny, well-drained, fairly moist soil.

Since Butterfly Bush needs to be planted in a well prepared hole, you might want to convince your parents to help you plant it. Most people love to watch butterflies, so begin by telling them how Butterfly Bush got its name. Every summer, Butterfly Bush sends up long stems which end in a colorful bundle of flowers. For butterflies, these flowers are tastier than ice cream. They love to land on Butterfly Bushes, and you will be sure to see them fluttering happily as they enjoy all the free dessert.

GARDEN SHRUB · ZONE 5-9

SPIDER FLOWER

(Cleome)

Spider Flower is a fast-growing plant with pink, rose, purple, white, or violet flowers. Their attractive flowers will continue blooming throughout the summer until winter finally arrives. Spider Flower grows four to five feet tall and likes a sunny, moist, well-drained place outside. Although it is an annual plant, new Spider Flowers usually grow each spring from seeds they dropped the year before.

Spider Flower got its name because its flowers have spidery legs sticking out all over. All these wavy spider-legs are called "stamens," and the Spider Flower stamens are three times as long as the petals. That's a lot longer than most other plants; check it out!

If you plant a bunch of Spider Flowers in one area, they will sway in the breeze and look especially spidery.

ANNUAL GARDEN PLANT

SPIDER LILY

(Hymenocallis)

Spider Lilies have big white flowers that bloom in the summer and can be six to eight inches across. The flowers have thin spidery legs arching out in all directions, which makes them look a little creepy. Spider Lilies like sunny places with at least half a day's worth of sunlight and well-drained soil.

Since Spider Lilies don't like the winter cold, it is a good idea to plant your Spider Lily bulbs in a pot or container once the weather becomes warm in the spring. That way you can grow your Spider Lily outside on a porch or patio for most of the year, and then when it gets cold, you can put the pot in a cool but not freezing place (maybe your garage) for the winter months.

**PERENNIAL GARDEN/
CONTAINER PLANT · ZONE 8-10**

SPIDER PLANT

(Chlorophytum comosum)

Spider Plant is a popular houseplant because it is very strong and grows well inside. It likes plenty of light, so you might want to keep yours next to a window. Let the soil of your Spider Plant dry a little bit before you water it again thoroughly. If your water has too much chlorine in it, your Spider Plant might have brown spots. Try spring water.

Spider Plant gets its name from the way little baby Spider Plants drop down on vines from the pot, much like a spider spins down from its web. These little Spider Plants can be removed and planted on their own to grow into a whole new plant.

There are all sorts of fun things you can do with your Spider Plant, like making a spider web out of yarn or string and hanging the little Spider Plants on it.

HOUSEPLANT

GOLDFISH PLANT

(Columnea)

Did you ever think you would see goldfish swimming around in the air? Well, you will if you grow a Goldfish Plant. The plant has leafy branches and forms beautiful orange/red flowers that look just like a goldfish swimming in mid-air!

Goldfish Plant is a viney houseplant that does best in a bright place with no direct sun. It would be great if you could grow yours in a hanging basket near a sunny window in your home. You can let the soil dry a little before watering, but remember to keep it misted with water. I think the orange/red flowers look most like goldfish when you look at them from the top.

HOUSEPLANT

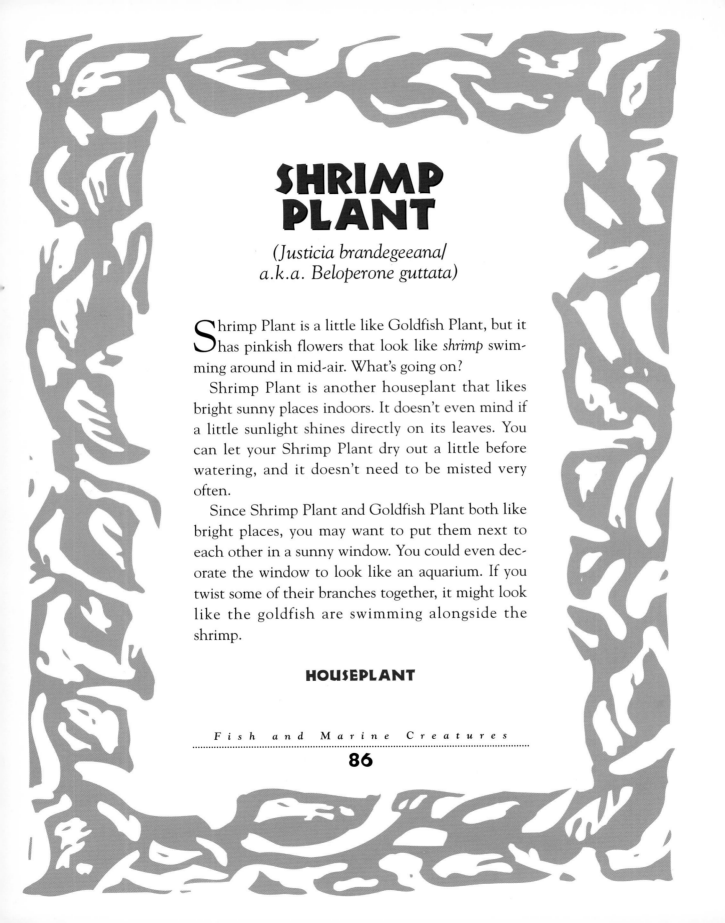

SHRIMP PLANT

(Justicia brandegeeana/
a.k.a. Beloperone guttata)

Shrimp Plant is a little like Goldfish Plant, but it has pinkish flowers that look like *shrimp* swimming around in mid-air. What's going on?

Shrimp Plant is another houseplant that likes bright sunny places indoors. It doesn't even mind if a little sunlight shines directly on its leaves. You can let your Shrimp Plant dry out a little before watering, and it doesn't need to be misted very often.

Since Shrimp Plant and Goldfish Plant both like bright places, you may want to put them next to each other in a sunny window. You could even decorate the window to look like an aquarium. If you twist some of their branches together, it might look like the goldfish are swimming alongside the shrimp.

HOUSEPLANT

TROUT LILY

(Erythronium)

Trout Lily likes the shade and got its nickname because the spots on its leaves make it look like a speckled trout. Trout Lily is sometimes found growing along the banks of streams, so whoever named it must have been thinking about fish!

Trout Lilies grow best in rich, moist soil in a shady or slightly sunny place. If you buy them as corms (a round thing like a bulb) and plant them in the fall, they will pop up ready to grow the following spring.

When people look at the Trout Lily, they see all kinds of different animals. Some of its other nicknames are Dog's Tooth Violet, Fawn Lily, and Adder's Tongue (an adder is a type of snake). What do *you* think it looks like?

PERENNIAL GARDEN PLANT · ZONE 3-8

LIFE IN A ZOO GARDEN

Now that you've read about all these animal plants, it's time to start your own Zoo Garden. But be careful: Life in a Zoo Garden can be pretty exciting. Just this morning, my cousin tried to pull my Donkey's Tail, my Butterfly Bush Airport had fifteen take-offs and landings in five minutes, my Elephant's Ear Plant needed a bath, and I counted three new piglets on my Piggyback Plant.

Then in the afternoon, a cat did five somersaults in my Catmint, a hummingbird and a bumblebee got in a fight over my Bee Balm, and my Spider Flower scared the mailman.

I wonder what's going to happen tomorrow. . . .

CROSS-REFERENCE

ZONE MAP
(SOURCE: USDA)

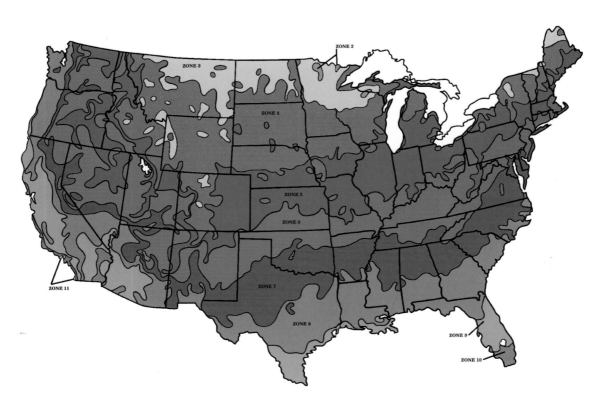

ZONE 2
ZONE 3
ZONE 4
ZONE 5
ZONE 6
ZONE 7
ZONE 8
ZONE 9
ZONE 10
ZONE 11

**Average annual
minimum temperature**

Temperature (°F)

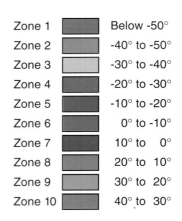

Zone 1		Below -50°
Zone 2		-40° to -50°
Zone 3		-30° to -40°
Zone 4		-20° to -30°
Zone 5		-10° to -20°
Zone 6		0° to -10°
Zone 7		10° to 0°
Zone 8		20° to 10°
Zone 9		30° to 20°
Zone 10		40° to 30°